A SPIRITUAL
CLEAR PURPOSE AND

BUILD
CREATE
DESIGN

Your Best Life Ever With God

JOE JOE DAWSON
Kingdom Mindset Mentor

Build Create Design: Your Best Life Ever with God

Copyright © 2024 by Joe Joe Dawson. All rights reserved. No part of this publication may be reproduced, distributed, or transmitted in any form or by any means, including photocopying, recording, or other electronic or mechanical methods, without the prior written permission of the copyright owner.

Contact Editor for permissions: joejoedawson@hotmail.com

Scriptures marked NKJV are taken from the NEW KING JAMES VERSION (NKJV): Scripture taken from the NEW KING JAMES VERSION®. Copyright© 1982 by Thomas Nelson, Inc. Used by permission. All rights reserved

Scriptures marked NLT are taken from the HOLY BIBLE, NEW LIVING TRANSLATION (NLT): Scriptures taken from the HOLY BIBLE, NEW LIVING TRANSLATION, Copyright©1996, 2004, 2007 by Tyndale House Foundation. Used by permission of Tyndale House Publishers, Inc., Carol Stream, Illinois 60188. All rights reserved. Used by permission.

Scriptures marked NIV are taken from the NEW INTERNATIONAL VERSION (NIV): Scripture taken from THE HOLY BIBLE, NEW INTERNATIONAL VERSION ®. Copyright©1973, 1978, 1984, 2011 by Biblica, Inc.™. Used by permission of Zondervan

All Scripture quotations are from The Passion Translation®. Copyright © 2017,2018, 2020 by Passion & Fire Ministries, Inc. Used by permission. All rights reserved. ThePassionTranslation.com.

www.joejoedawson.net

Do You Need Prayer?

If you would like prayer for anything,
just click the Contact Button on our website.

JoeJoeDawson.net

I would love to pray with you.

I dedicate this book to TheDawson5:
Autumn, Malachi, Judah, and Ezra.

Individually,
we're doing exploits for the Kingdom.

And together,
we're building great things for God.

Keep building, creating, and designing for Him!

Note from the Author

Build it. It's been long enough.

You've been talking about it, thinking about it, and putting it off.

When will you build what you've been seeing in your mind?

God gave you the vision—your purpose, your calling, your destiny. You've been telling everyone how great it's going to be, but when will you actually start building it?

Now is the time.

When God imparts something to your spirit, it's because He needs it accomplished on the Earth.

Quit acting like it's optional!

It's time to throw caution to the wind and do what He's called you to do.

Now.

Maybe your mind has been limiting you, talking you out of great ideas, and feeding you reasons why it won't work.

But God promises to make a way where there seems to be no way (Isaiah 43:19).

If you'll step out in faith, the right team, the right finances, and the right opportunities will come your way. Everything will fall into place.

But He's expecting you to go for it.

So go!

If you've been waiting for permission, here it is. Take the limits off your thinking and DO what God has placed in your heart.

It's time to build.

Joe Joe Dawson

Table of Contents

BUILD

Chapter 1: The Answer: Build — 15

Chapter 2: Do the Work — 21

Chapter 3: A Kingdom Mindset — 29

Chapter 4: Wise People Build — 39

CREATE

Chapter 5: God's Creative Word — 49

Chapter 6: Hear a Word, Build a Word — 57

DESIGN

Chapter 7: You Need a Design! — 67

Chapter 8: Details, Details, Details — 75

WITH GOD

Chapter 9: It's Time for Breakthrough — 87

Chapter 10: Acceleration — 95

BUILD

No one's coming to rescue you; No one's coming to make everything work out. You have to take responsibility for your own life.

CHAPTER 1

THE ANSWER: BUILD

It's time, it's time, it's time – it's time to build.

Recently, in prayer, the Lord told me, "Tell the people they're going to build themselves out of this." He repeated, "They're going to BUILD themselves out of this."

"Okay, God, I'll tell them," I said.

There was only one problem—I had no idea what 'this' was!

Then it hit me. It's different for everyone.

Some people are struggling with their health.

Some are struggling with their mindset or emotions.

Some are struggling with their relationships.

Some are struggling with their finances.

Whatever 'this' is for you, here's God's answer for how you'll get out of your situation—you're going to BUILD.

If your relationship with God isn't strong, you will build yourself out of it by reading your Bible daily, having regular prayer time, and letting the Lord speak to you.

If your health isn't where you want it to be, you will build yourself out of it by getting serious about new habits.

If your finances aren't in the best shape, you will get an advisor and begin strategically handling your money.

In other words, you'll stop waiting for someone to rescue you and start taking responsibility for your own life.

People pray and expect God to do something big for them, but they're only willing to do a little bit themselves.

But the solution to every problem has a "God" part and a "you" part. You've got to pray like it all depends on God, and work like it all depends on you.

I talk to a lot of people. These are the kinds of things I hear.

"I don't have any friends."

Well, the Bible says, "A man who has friends must himself be friendly..." (Proverbs 18:24 NKJV).

When was the last time you asked someone out for lunch or to have a coffee?

If you want to develop relationships, you have to reach out to others. You can't wait for them to come to you.

"The Lord said He's going to bring finances into my family."

Okay, so what are you doing extra? Have you got a side business going? Are you tithing and sowing seed? When was the last time you helped a neighbor?

Proverbs 11:25 says, "The generous will prosper…" (NLT). If you're not prospering, there may be a reason!

"God said He's going to save my family!"

Great! When did you last talk with one of your family members about the Lord? Have you shared a scripture or a testimony about what He's doing in your life or invited a relative to church? God will move on them when you move! Stop waiting!

One person told me about a ministry God put on their heart:

"Joe Joe, I want to help the homeless community."

"Awesome. I've got a friend with a ministry called Church Under the Bridge. We buy breakfast and serve it to the homeless."

The person responded, "I feel so relieved; I'll give you $20 toward it!"

I answered, "Oh, no, you won't! You're going to pitch in $50 AND come with us!"

Over and over, I hear sincere people say, "The Lord said, the Lord said, the Lord said . . ." but only a few people are stepping out to do something about the words they hear.

Stop and take a good look at your life right now. Think about your walk with God, your marriage, kids, health, finances, business, or ministry.

God has provided a clear answer for any negative situation you may find yourself in.

If you want out of it, you've got to build.

Reflection

_____
_____
_____
_____
_____
_____
_____
_____
_____
_____

Scriptures to Think About

Matthew 7:24-27 NKJV

Therefore whoever hears these sayings of Mine, and does them, I will liken him to a wise man who built his house on the rock: and the rain descended, the floods came, and the winds blew and beat on that house; and it did not fall, for it was founded on the rock.

But everyone who hears these sayings of Mine, and does not do them, will be like a foolish man who built his house on the sand: and the rain descended, the floods came, and the winds blew and beat on that house; and it fell. And great was its fall.

Proverbs 14:1 NLT

A wise woman builds her home, but a foolish woman tears it down with her own hands.

1 Corinthians 3:10 NIV

By the grace God has given me, I laid a foundation as a wise builder, and someone else is building on it. But each one should build with care.

Your life will get exciting when you start aggressively pursuing what God has called you to do.

CHAPTER 2

DO THE WORK

When people tell me about their dreams, visions, and what they want to do with their lives, I get excited!

But when I ask, "What are you doing about them?" I'm often disappointed by what I hear. Most of them aren't doing anything to pursue what's in their hearts.

I mean, if you genuinely want to lead people to the Lord, why don't you just wake up and say, "I'm going to lead somebody to the Lord today," and trust God to put someone in your path?

Your life will get exciting when you start aggressively pursuing what God has called you to do. When you start building, everything will change.

You may have to start small, but you need to start somewhere!

When my wife and I first married, the Lord told us to build our finances. We were able to put a whopping $50 a month into savings. $50 a month, woohoo!

When I started to build my early-morning prayer life, I could pray for four and a half minutes. After that, I was out of things to pray about. Now I pray for an hour and a half and think, "Oh, man, is it over? It feels like we just got started."

I've watched people start working out at the gym. They'll hit it hard for ten minutes and then complain, "I need an energy drink. I'm tired!" No, you've got to hang in there and get those reps in! You have to build yourself up!

When we started buying rental houses, we started with one. One. Then it was two, and suddenly, it was five! Today, I don't even know how many we own.

You see? It doesn't matter how small the beginning step is—you must start moving.

Many people don't want to build, but the Lord said that's what you need to do. You must build your way OUT of wherever you are and INTO wherever God has called you to be.

God's not calling you into something that you're already doing. He's calling you into something you will have to build by faith.

But the good news is this: there's no limit on how much you can build. You are the only one who determines where you stop. Pause for a minute and think about that.

There's no limit to the souls you can lead to the Lord.

There's no limit to the number of people you can get healed.

There's no limit to the amount of finances you can make.

You are the only limit in the equation because God is limitless.

I hear many people complain, "I don't know why things aren't working out in my life."

I'll tell you a secret. If you sit down with someone with a building mentality, they'll be able to tell you why.

I was talking to someone about a new project the other day, and they outdreamed me, like, way, way outdreamed me. I thought to myself, "How are you outdreaming me?"

They said, "Oh, Mr. Dawson, I think you could . . ." and started rattling off ideas!

Everything can shift quickly when you're around someone who starts talking like that. Things can get better really fast.

When I mentor someone, I always ask, "What if you are limiting yourself? What if there's really no limit to what you can do?"

Then, I challenge them to try to name one area of their life that can't be improved. They never can.

Every day, I pray that my walk with God gets stronger, that my marriage gets stronger, that my relationship with my kids gets stronger, that my businesses get stronger, that my ministry gets stronger, and that my mindset gets stronger!

A weak mindset is the number one thing that stops people from moving forward with their dreams.

The Bible says, "The spirit indeed is willing, but the flesh is weak" (Matthew 26:41 NKJV). Your spirit wants to go for whatever God says; your mind causes the blockage.

It's pretty simple to understand. Your mind controls your body. If your mind says, "Foot, move to the right," then your foot moves to the right. If your mind says, "Foot, move to the left," then your foot moves to the left. Your body does whatever your mind tells it to do.

But what if you could train your mind to do what your spirit says? What if you could make it cooperate with your spirit like your foot cooperates with your mind? It's possible!

When God drops a dream into your heart, your spirit believes it. It wants to forge ahead and do what God says! It's your mind that makes you doubt it's possible.

Four times in the New Testament, it says, "With men this is impossible, but with God all things are possible" (Matthew 19:26 NIV).

If you meditate on that verse long enough and confess it loudly enough, you'll eventually convince your mind to believe it.

And if your mind believes it, it won't be hard to act on it!

That's why learning to control your MINDSET is so important. You've got to stop making excuses.

It sounds so holy to say, "Give me some time to pray about it. Let me see if the Lord's in it."

When someone tells me they need to pray about something, I usually say, "The Holy Ghost and I talk regularly. I know His voice. I don't have to pray and fast for three days to hear Him."

In Jeremiah 33:3, God promises, "Call to Me, and I will answer you" (NKJV). You don't call somebody on the phone and wait three days for them to answer, do you?

When you make a point to talk to God on a regular basis, you'll find out that He's talkative—and He answers fast!

You'll be able to move straight into what He has for you.

Other people tell me, "I can't do it now. I'll do it later." I don't know where you live, but here in East Texas, "later" means never! When God calls you to do something, you've got to respond now. You can't wait until later.

If you pray and hear a word from God, but you don't do anything with that word, the Bible says you're just fooling yourself. James 1:22 warns us, "Do not merely listen to the word, and so deceive yourselves. Do what it says" (NIV).

If you look at our world today, you'll see many people who are being deceived because they're hearing God's words without applying what they hear.

When you aggressively act on what God puts in your heart, He will blow you out of the water with what He can do. So pray like it all depends on God—because it does—and work like it all depends on you—because it does.

Do the work, friend. Just do the work.

Reflection

_____
_____
_____
_____
_____
_____
_____

Scriptures to Think About

Matthew 26:41 NKJV
Watch and pray lest you enter into temptation. The spirit indeed is willing, but the flesh is weak.

Matthew 19:26 NIV

Jesus looked at them and said, "With man this is impossible, but with God all things are possible."

Jeremiah 33:3 NKJV

'Call to Me, and I will answer you, and show you great and mighty things, which you do not know.'

James 1:22 NIV

Do not merely listen to the word, and so deceive yourselves. Do what it says.

*You can spend

your whole life helping

everybody else

and never do

what you're called to do.*

CHAPTER 3

A KINGDOM MINDSET

You have to build with a Kingdom mindset to have lasting success. You can't build on YOUR desires; you have to build on HIS desires.

At first, I usually don't want to do what God puts on my heart. I might think, *I don't have a degree for this. I'm not trained.*

But, you see, I don't have to AGREE with what He wants me to do; I just have to DO it.

I have to act on what I know He's telling me in the spirit and IGNORE my mind and emotions.

The Lord told me, "I don't need you to have a degree; I don't need you to be trained. I just need you to be obedient. I can show you how to do anything."

Maybe you don't want to write books or create videos or preach like I do. Perhaps you don't even want to invite people over for dinner. But it's not about you! Who said it was about you?

The Word says, "Take up your cross daily" (Luke 9:23 NLT).

What is the cross? It's the place where we let OUR desires die so we can fulfill HIS. It's the place where we decide we are going to do what He tells us to do.

Colossians 3:23-24 says, "And whatever you do, do it heartily, as unto the Lord and not to men, knowing that from the Lord, you'll receive the reward of the inheritance; for you serve the Lord Christ" (NKJV).

Many times on social media, someone will leave a nasty comment about a video or something I write.

I just think, "It ain't for you; you ain't my people! But a lot of other people out there like it!"

When doing things for God, you don't have to worry about what someone says about you. You don't have to worry about what ANYONE thinks.

They don't sign your paychecks!

When you act on what God puts in your heart, you work for the Kingdom of God. People may not like what you do, but if you ignore them and keep going, you'll see KINGDOM results.

I can't tell you how many people I've seen healed on the street or at a store following this advice.

I always ask people needing healing, "Do you know anything about the Lord?"

Some do, but others respond, "No, man, I'm not into that."

I answer, "I didn't ask you if you were into it. I asked if you want to be healed! You may not be into Him, but He's into you!"

Often, they don't want to talk about Jesus, but they DO want healing! So, after they get healed, I just keep talking.

I say, "Look! Your limp is gone; where'd your limp go? Whenever I get a miracle, I think about Jesus! Why don't you think about Him, too, because He's the one who sent me in your direction today!"

Never let anybody talk you out of doing what God puts in your heart.

You might look at someone and think, "There's no way they'll receive their healing," but God's thinking, "I'm just looking for somebody wild enough to lay hands on them."

It doesn't just apply to healing, either.

One time, I was standing behind an elderly lady at the bank. She thought she had a hundred dollars in her savings, but the teller told her she was mistaken. She really needed the money.

I overheard the conversation and felt led to give her a hundred dollars out of my account.

When you're running with God, He'll put things in your heart that make no sense to your natural mind, but you should do them anyway!

Another time, I was talking to a sweet little lady watching one of our video programs.

She said, "I'm 82 years old."

I responded, "Okay, cool, young lady. You're 82."

She told me, "I've always helped in the church. I've always served."

I said, "Yes, ma'am, you've helped and served. That's great. You're 82, and you've helped people."

"Yeah."

I asked, "What have you done for God? What are you CALLED to do?"

She hesitated and said, "Whoa, whoa! He gave me some lofty things to do multiple times."

It turns out that this sweet 82-year-old lady had never done ANYTHING the Lord told her to do! She just ran to the church and helped.

Now, we need the gifts of helps and administration; it's Biblical (1 Corinthians 12:28), but she never actually did anything God called her to do.

She admitted, "I'm so broke. I didn't get much Social Security or retirement pay because I was busy helping everybody else."

I said, "It's commendable to help; we're supposed to help people."

But now she feels like she did nothing with her life.

So, I started helping her dream! At 82, she had never dreamed!

I explained that during Bible days, if a shepherd lost a lamb, he would go to the Lord and say, "Here is a leg, here is an ear. I fought. I lost, but I fought." (Amos 3:12)

I encouraged her, "Do SOMETHING. God will honor it."

She wanted to go on a mission trip.

I said, "Good! Get yourself a passport. Raise some money. Go on that mission trip!"

She got excited but then said, "But I'm broke."

"Let's pray," I told her. "God owns the cattle on a thousand hills" (Psalm 50:10).

Being from Texas, I get excited about that verse! My earthly father had a sale barn where cattle would be auctioned off. If God's got cattle, He can sell them, so finances are unlimited for the work of the Kingdom of God!

If God calls you to start a ministry, what you need will be there! If He calls you to step out into a big business venture, the money will be there.

This unlimited supply is in more than just the area of finances too! Have you ever started witnessing to someone when, all of a sudden, you sound like Billy Graham? Words just fly out of your mouth.

You might think to yourself, "Man, that was good! I don't know where that came from!"

It came from God! He just needed someone to step out in faith and do His Kingdom work in that situation.

As we ended the conversation, the sweet little lady asked me, "How come nobody ever taught me this? I've been in the church my whole life."

I responded, "I've been in the church for a long time, too, but now I'm in the Kingdom. We think differently in the Kingdom."

Don't take me wrong, but you can spend your whole life helping everybody else and never do what you're called to do.

You can spend your whole life scared, never acting on what God has put in your heart.

I encourage you to be ALL IN and to DO the works of the Kingdom, showing the love of God to people who need it.

I've never forgotten when I was about 24, and the Lord told me to witness to a big biker dude sitting in the parking lot of a convenience store.

Instead of walking over to him right then, I decided I'd go into the store, get what I needed, and witness to him when I came back out.

However, when I opened the door to the store, I glanced back, and he was already gone!

I asked God, "Why didn't I act when You first told me to?"

And I promised Him right then and there to never hesitate again when I feel prompted to strike up a conversation or pray for someone.

If God puts something on my heart now, I do it immediately.

Having a Kingdom mindset changes everything.

Reflection

Scriptures to Think About

Luke 9:23 NLT

Then he said to the crowd, "If any of you wants to be my follower, you must give up your own way, take up your cross daily, and follow me."

Colossians 3:23-24 NKJV

And whatever you do, do it heartily, as to the Lord and not to men, knowing that from the Lord you will receive the reward of the inheritance; for you serve the Lord Christ.

Luke 2:49 NKJV

And He said to them, "Why did you seek Me? Did you not know that I must be about My Father's business?"

Matthew 6:33 NLT

Seek the Kingdom of God above all else, and live righteously, and he will give you everything you need.

Psalm 50:10 NKJV

For every beast of the forest is Mine,
And the cattle on a thousand hills.

You start by building

your relationship with God,

but then you must build

in the world around you.

CHAPTER 4

WISE PEOPLE BUILD

So, what do you need to build in your life?

The first thing you need to build is your relationship with God.

Consistency is key with God. He loves consistency. Whether you pray every morning or stay available whenever He nudges you to do something, be dependable.

When you are steady in your relationship with Him, He'll show you how to build the Kingdom!

The first thing God ever told me to build was my prayer life. I was around 20 years old, and there was no one at church close to my age, so I asked for a key and prayed in the sanctuary for three to five hours each night.

I had no friends, but Jesus became my best friend! I built a solid relationship with Him, and I'm still standing on that strong foundation today!

You start by building your relationship with God, but then you must build in the world around you.

"Wise people are builders — they build families, businesses, communities" (Proverbs 24:3 TPT).

Wise people build families.

I told God I wanted to marry the greatest person in the world.

Then I found Autumn.

My friends told me, "You don't have a shot. Girls like her don't marry guys like you."

But my God is the God of the impossible!

"She's got to marry somebody," I told them, "Why not me?"

I married her, and she's still the love of my life to this day.

Sometimes, people ask me, "What about your kids? Do you ever worry about them making wrong decisions?"

No. When they ask me why not, I explain, "Because God and Autumn and I are good parents. We follow the Bible and listen to the Holy Spirit."

We've built something good with our family, and when you build something good, you have confidence that it will stand firm.

Wise people build businesses.

Did you notice that the word "business" in that verse is plural? It says businesses, not just business.

Once you get a business going, it's easy to start two, three, or four! Once you learn how to build, you can keep on building.

My dad built a bunch of businesses. He was a cattle farmer, but he also had a sale barn, a cattle-hauling truck business, and several other ventures with different business partners.

"Why do you have so many?" I asked him.

He explained, "Son, if one stream stops, it doesn't matter; the other streams can still feed the river. If a second stream dries up, it's still okay; I'll always have enough streams to keep the river from running dry."

Dad sowed out of all those businesses, too. He'd pick up one of his business checkbooks and write a check to Billy Graham. Oh, how he loved Billy! Then he'd pick up his next business checkbook and write another.

I finally asked, "Dad, how many checks will you write to him?"

He said, "Well, son, these checkbooks are all from different businesses, and I want ALL my businesses blessed. I invest in Billy because the man's winning souls."

That's how Dad built his businesses. That's how he prospered.

Wise people also build communities.

Communities are just groups of people who are like-minded. You're probably part of several communities.

You might be part of a ladies' group that sells plasticware or a health group where everyone follows the same program.

If your kids are into sports or some other kind of school activity, you belong to that community too.

Do you realize it's possible to build in those communities? All you need is a Kingdom mindset!

When you walk out the door in the morning, you should think, "I'm going to prophesy to someone today; I'm going to see somebody healed; I'm going to be the voice in someone's life that will shift everything."

It can all happen right there in your communities! You can build the Kingdom of God.

Now, the very last part of Proverbs 23:4 says, "And through intelligence and insight, their enterprises are established, and they endure" (TPT).

I'm declaring over you that what you build this year will endure!

I don't care if you built something in the past that failed. I don't care if you started a business that went bankrupt. I don't care if you've had a relationship that's been rocky.

This year, things are going to be different. This year will be the year everything turns out right!

Wise people are builders.

Is building hard? Yeah, it's hard, but it's fun! Who wants an easy life? When all is said and done, will you feel satisfied with EASY?

Let's be wise people and build.

Reflection

Scriptures to Think About

Proverbs 24:3 TPT

Wise people are builders — they build families, businesses, communities. And through intelligence and insight their enterprises are established and endure.

Proverbs 24:3 NKJV

Through wisdom a house is built,
And by understanding it is established.

1 Corinthians 3:9-10 NKJV

For we are God's fellow workers; you are God's field, you are God's building. According to the grace of God which was given to me, as a wise master builder I have laid the foundation, and another builds on it. But let each one take heed how he builds on it.

Romans 12:2 NKJV

And do not be conformed to this world, but be transformed by the renewing of your mind, that you may prove what is that good and acceptable and perfect will of God.

CREATE

Your current mood is a result of what you've been saying over the past few days.

Your current circumstances reflect the decisions you've made for the past few years.

CHAPTER 5

GOD'S CREATIVE WORD

You've got to fall in love with God's Word and learn to speak it over your life! If you're not already in love with the Bible, pray this prayer:

God, I pray that I love your Word, that I absolutely love your Word, and that when I read it, it comes alive to me.

The prophet Jeremiah was in love with His Word like that.

He said, "When I discovered your words, I devoured them. They are my joy and my heart's delight, for I bear your name, O Lord God of Heaven's Armies" (Jeremiah 15:16 NLT).

The Bible holds the secrets to your best life ever, so you should learn to love it like Jeremiah did.

You should also learn to love God's presence. When people are backsliding or no longer feeling passionate about God, it's because they're not spending enough time in His presence. The more time you spend with Him, the deeper you'll fall in love with Him.

As a bonus, you'll end up acting like He acts, feeling what He feels, and speaking His words!

Without God, people tend to speak negatively, but the Bible tells us, "The tongue can bring death or life; those who love to talk will reap the consequences" (Proverbs 18:21 NLT).

In our house, if one of us accidentally says something negative, we rebuke it. We don't allow ourselves to confess negativity. Sometimes I slip up, but I'll correct myself immediately by declaring, "I rebuke those negative words."

So many people are moved by their emotions or how they feel physically. I might wake up with a sinus headache, but I won't let my body decide what words I will speak or control what I do that day!

I've never read in the Bible that Jesus woke up and said to the disciples, "Boys, take a couple of days off. I'm not feeling my best today. I think I need a break." No, Jesus got up early EVERY day and prayed because he had important things to do.

So, why is it so easy to say negative words? Most negative words are inspired by FEAR. But fear doesn't come from God—it comes from the enemy!

John 10:10 tells us, "The thief does not come except to

steal, and to kill, and to destroy. I have come that they may have life, and that they may have it more abundantly" (NKJV).

If you're worried because you've gotten a bad doctor's report, you need to rebuke that fear!

Say, "Excuse me, but my body is the temple of the Holy Spirit! You have no right to stay here." Pray against the root cause of the problem, and God will show you what to do about it.

Sometimes, it may be something natural; sometimes, it might be something supernatural; just follow His word and don't overthink it.

I remember one time I was sick for a while, but the Lord told me I was going to be healed. I thought it was going to be by someone laying hands on me, but instead, He said, "Go have emergency surgery."

I thought, "Oh, man, that's not what I expected!" The plan worked out great, but it wasn't what I thought.

Another time, I had already decided, "Man, I need to go to the doctor," but I got a supernatural touch! It doesn't always happen the way you think.

The wildest story happened before I was married when I tried to look big and strong for Autumn! I was working out in the gym a lot and gave myself a hernia. It hurt so badly, but an intercessor told me, "Quit grappling about it!" She slapped my stomach, and the hernia went back in!

Friend, God hears you when you pray and has a plan for your victory. You've got to recognize that when fear comes in, it's just the enemy trying to mess with your mind.

2 Timothy 1:7 says, "For God has not given us a spirit of fear, but of power and of love and of a sound mind" (NKJV).

Your mind needs to be SOUND to hear God's words in every situation you may face. You can't respond emotionally; you've got to have self-control. Self-control means not getting emotional when fear barges its way through the door.

When something bad happens, just say, "I'll process this information without getting emotional, and then I'll deal with the enemy. Fear, you sit down and shut up; I'll get back to you in a minute!"

You have authority over the enemy; he doesn't have authority over you. Fear doesn't pay rent, so kick it out of your house!

You really need three friends you can call at any time to pray for you when you're under attack. There's nothing like having good friends who will cover you.

If you don't have those kinds of friends yet, then BE that kind of friend. Sow your prayers for others as seeds, and God will send you a harvest of people who will do the same for you. That's the way the Kingdom works!

Even your everyday words are seeds that will produce a good harvest or a bad one. If you're unsure what to say, take the safe route and sow God's Word; it has the creative power to change your thoughts and life.

Romans 12:2 says, "And do not be conformed to this world, but be transformed by the renewing of your mind, that you may prove what is that good and acceptable and perfect will of God" (NKJV).

God's Word is so creative that it can transform your thinking and bring you into an amazing place—the perfect will of God.

If a stranger walked up to me and asked me what I wanted to do with my life, I'd say, "I'd want to do exactly what I'm doing right now!" I wouldn't add or take away anything. I'm in the perfect place because I'm doing exactly what I'm called to do.

How long did it take to get to that place, Joe Joe?

I don't measure it by time; I measure it by decisions. It took a lot of good decisions to get me to where I am today.

If you want to move into a better place in life, here's what you should do. For your next five big decisions—not decisions about where you're going to go to lunch but decisions that affect the Kingdom—be sure you make the RIGHT decisions, and your life will change forever. What you say and what you do are the Bible's keys to success.

Proverbs 12:14 sums it up best: "From the fruit of their lips people are filled with good things, and the work of their hands brings them reward" (NIV).

What you say today will manifest in your tomorrow. Your current mood is a result of what you've been saying over the past few days. Your current circumstances reflect the decisions you've made for the past few years.

I used to be negative, critical, and angry, but it got me nowhere. I used to make bad decisions, but I quickly learned that they didn't take me where I wanted to go. I'm done with that kind of life. God's Word has taught me to focus on the best that could happen in every situation, and that's what I go for in word and deed—God's best.

Reflection

_____
_____
_____
_____
_____
_____

Scriptures to Think About

Jeremiah 15:16 NLT

When I discovered your words, I devoured them.
They are my joy and my heart's delight,
for I bear your name,
O Lord God of Heaven's Armies.

Proverbs 18:21 NLT

The tongue can bring death or life;
those who love to talk will reap the consequences.

John 10:10 NKJV

The thief does not come except to steal, and to kill, and to destroy. I have come that they may have life, and that they may have it more abundantly.

2 Timothy 1:7 NKJV

For God has not given us a spirit of fear, but of power and of love and of a sound mind.

Proverbs 12:14 NIV

From the fruit of their lips people are filled with good things, and the work of their hands brings them reward.

*When God puts an idea

in your heart,

you must stop looking at it

like it's optional.*

CHAPTER 6

HEAR A WORD, BUILD A WORD

My wife and I are continually creating everything from businesses to ministries. We're creative people: prophetic and apostolic. We hear a word, and then we build the word.

As I kept praying recently, the Lord began speaking to me about how many people are sitting on prophetic words from Him: creative ideas, dreams, and visions from the Lord for the future.

These words are important for two reasons. One, they need to be done for God's Kingdom purposes for the future. Two, a lot of people's finances are tied to the visions He gives.

A buddy of mine called me one day, just distraught. He said, "Joe Joe, I've been with this organization for years, and the company just told us they're downsizing by 15%."

My friend thought, "I've been here for 20 years. I'm safe."

Nope. The company cut everyone who had been there 15 years or longer. They wanted to go in a fresh direction and didn't want any seasoned veterans around, especially those getting close to retirement age.

He asked me, "What do I do now?"

I answered, "You create. You verbally bless the company for employing you for 20 years, but now it's time to create what's in your heart."

He said, "It's funny you say that because I have so much in my heart, but I just didn't want to do it."

"Well, now your back's against the wall. You have to do it."

When God puts an idea in your heart, you must stop looking at it like it's optional. God doesn't sit around in Heaven, thinking, "I'll give them my opinion and let them choose whether or not they want to do it."

When God gives you a vision, it means He chose YOU out of everybody on the planet to carry it out.

Every book I've ever written was because God wanted me to write that book. He spoke the idea to me, and I picked up the pen.

You see a lot of people in life who create amazing businesses. They may not even be believers, but I'm confident God gave them a vision. He gave them a dream.

I've heard people who claim to be atheists say, "I had

a dream about starting this business. It was the most miraculous, majestic dream." I think, "That was God."

God gave it to that person because they have tenacity: He knew they'd push through and do it.

Why do a lot of worldly people succeed? Because they rely on their God-given talent and ability 100%. They work like it all depends on THEM.

But what if the children of God worked like it all depended on them AND prayed like it all depended on God? That combination would create supernatural success!

Many people want God to do everything while they stay lazy. But God's not calling lazy people.

He doesn't present you with an idea and say, "Here, I'm giving you this great idea. I'll do 90% of it, and you just kind of work 30 minutes a day, and you'll have everything you need in life."

That's not what the Bible teaches. The Bible promotes a strong work ethic: "If a man doesn't work, a man doesn't eat" (2 Thessalonians 3:10 NIV).

Everybody wants free money, but that's not Biblical. People want success without doing the work. Yes, God will bless and multiply your efforts, but you've got to be creative, especially when times are tough!

I know many people in the church and business worlds who get caught off guard when something bad happens.

They lose a job. A new law is put in place. A corporation downsizes or gets bought out. Yes, a whole corporation!

I know a bunch of guys who worked at a factory. They all called me on the same day, scared out of their minds.

I said, "What happened?"

They told me, "Man, they got this new technology that can do the work of three men – flawless, no mistakes. And they'll make back the money they paid for the machine in just two years IF they release three guys. And the machine has a 5-year warranty! Joe Joe, we're about to lose our jobs!"

What you've got to understand is that the world is changing. Innovation is changing. You've got to create because when you create something God has called you to create, it's YOURS. It's yours and God's, and no one can take that away.

I was part of a church ministry, spent years building it, and one day, the head pastor came to me and said, "Your time here is done." Okay, you're the head pastor, and what you say goes. My time is done.

Back then, there was no Joe Joe Dawson Ministries. I was

just a ministry under the umbrella of a church, and after eight or so years, I was removed. I had never created anything for myself.

When I was a little kid, people would say, "Go get a job at this post office, at this factory, at this mill, at this company, at this place, or that place. Work there for 40 years and retire."

You don't see many people retiring anymore. I was talking to a gentleman the other day—a great guy, 70 years old.

He said, "Joe, I've always worked hard, but I've never worked in the same job for over eight years because things were always changing." Sadly, this guy never created anything for himself, either.

What has God put inside of you? Has He put a business idea, an idea for a book, or a ministry in your heart? What has He put inside of you, and what will YOU do with it?

The world is changing at a rapid pace. People message me daily because something changes, and they have no idea what to do.

But the people who have learned to create just jump in and start fresh! They pivot. They embrace new technology because they know that with innovation, they can build quicker than they've ever built before.

You can do that too. I encourage you to create!

What desires has God put in your heart?

Many people want to create extra finances to support the next generation.

Proverbs 13:22 says, "A good man leaves an inheritance to his children's children" (NKJV).

But someone must CREATE that inheritance!

There are many opportunities out there just waiting for you to act on them.

Hear a word, build the word.

Create.

Reflection

_____
_____
_____
_____
_____
_____
_____
_____

Scripture to Think About

Proverbs 13:22 NLT

A good man leaves an inheritance to his children's children, But the wealth of the sinner is stored up for the righteous.

Ecclesiastes 9:10 NLT

Whatever you do, do well. For when you go to the grave, there will be no work or planning or knowledge or wisdom.

Proverbs 22:29 NIV

Do you see someone skilled in their work? They will serve before kings; they will not serve before officials of low rank.

Genesis 1:1 NKJV

In the beginning God created the heavens and the earth.

Genesis 1:27 NKJV

So God created man in His own image; in the image of God He created him; male and female He created them.

DESIGN

Now that you have a prophetic word from God, you need to design your time around it.

CHAPTER 7

YOU NEED A DESIGN!

Have you ever noticed how specific God's Word is?

God gave Noah precise measurements to build the ark.

He told the children of Israel exactly how many times to walk around Jericho's walls and when to blow their trumpets and shout.

The wise men followed a particular star that led them right to the Christ.

Every time God gives you a vision, He has a specific DESIGN in mind for you to bring that vision to pass. Without those specifics, there may be delays, hardships, and even failure.

Noah had a creative, prophetic word to build the ark, but how would that boat would have turned out if he just started throwing any old wood together without a plan?

What if the children of Israel marched around the city only three times? Would the walls of Jericho have ever fallen?

And would the wise men from the East have ever found

Jesus if they hadn't followed the star?

In the New Testament, Jesus tells a story about a person who doesn't plan out a design for his project. Instead, he just starts stacking bricks!

> But don't begin until you count the cost. For who would begin construction of a building without first calculating the cost to see if there is enough money to finish it? Otherwise, you might complete only the foundation before running out of money, and then everyone would laugh at you. They would say, 'There's the person who started that building and couldn't afford to finish it!'
>
> Or what king would go to war against another king without first sitting down with his counselors to discuss whether his army of 10,000 could defeat the 20,000 soldiers marching against him? And if he can't, he will send a delegation to discuss terms of peace while the enemy is still far away.
>
> —Luke 14:28-32 NLT

Wouldn't it be embarrassing to share the vision the Lord has put in your heart, start on the project, and NOT be able to complete it? Some of you have faced that situation, but I'm here to give you hope.

Now you know what part of the plan you were missing—a design!

Let's focus in on the word "design."

Design means to plan, draw out, or produce something tangible from a vision.

The Lord wants you to meditate on how that word He has given to you will come to life. How are you going to accomplish it? How will you BUILD what He's told you to build?

Instead of seeking the Lord for a design to make an idea happen, most people are waiting for Him to bring it to pass Himself.

Conference junkies run with their tape recorders from place to place, but they never seek the Lord for designs for the prophetic words they hear. They love to listen to all the great things God wants them to do, but what happens to those prophecies after they get home?

Do they ever get transcribed where they can be read and prayed over? Or do they sit in their voice memos for months or years—and eventually get deleted?

You need to shake the dust off all those creative words you've gotten from the God, and seek Him about how to bring them to pass.

The prophetic words we receive are to be our guiding light—like a lighthouse beckoning to a ship out at sea.

But the ship's captain still has the responsibility to plot the ship's course so that it will arrive safely at its desired destination.

Once you have a creative word from God, it is your responsibility to seek God for the design. The Holy Spirit will guide you, but YOUR hands must stay firmly grasped on the boatwheel!

But that's not the only thing you need a design for! You also need one for your everyday life!

Before I go to bed each night, I know what I'll wear tomorrow. I know what I'll eat for breakfast. I know what I'm going to do throughout my day.

The first thing I do each morning is get a cup of coffee and walk straight to my prayer chair. It just works for me—one hand raised to the Lord and the other wrapped around the handle of my coffee cup!

Later, I get ready and drop my son off at school. The trip gives us time to connect.

After that, I head straight to the church to pray a little more and read my Bible. It's part of the plan.

I have two other books that I read every day, too. They sit in particular place on my desk. It's all part of my morning routine.

Then I get to work. My day is already planned on my calendar. I know what I will do each hour—what calls I will make for mentoring and health coaching, what videos I will shoot, and what books I will work on.

Several times a day, I stop and talk to my wife. She's the love of my life. My day is designed around her.

When my workday ends, I go home and eat dinner with my family. Autumn's a great cook, and I look forward to hearing about everyone's day.

You may say, "That's nice for you, but I don't do structure."

Oh, really? Don't you eat lunch at the same time every day? What time do you go to bed or when do you wake up? And I know you go to your favorite restaurant every Friday night!

Everyone has some sort of structure.

But now that you have a prophetic word from God, you need to design your time around it.

The Holy Spirit will help you create a design for your day with your most important goals in mind. When you have this, you will be able to build faster and more effectively than you ever have before!

Reflection

Scriptures to Think About

Luke 14:28-32 NLT

But don't begin until you count the cost. For who would begin construction of a building without first calculating the cost to see if there is enough money to finish it? Otherwise, you might complete only the foundation before running out of money, and then everyone would laugh at you. They would say, 'There's the person who started that building and couldn't afford to finish it!'

Or what king would go to war against another king without first sitting down with his counselors to discuss whether his army of 10,000 could defeat the 20,000 soldiers marching against him? And if he can't, he will send a delegation to discuss terms of peace while the enemy is still far away.

Matthew 7:24-27 NKJV

Therefore whoever hears these sayings of Mine, and does them, I will liken him to a wise man who built his house on the rock: and the rain descended, the floods came, and the winds blew and beat on that house; and it did not fall, for it was founded on the rock.

You can be confident you'll get the details for your plan by spending time with God.

CHAPTER 8

GET THE DETAILS!

My son Ezra is eleven, but he already has a vision for being financially successful.

He tells me, "Dad, when I turn eighteen, I want to be able to..." and then he starts naming things he wants to fund. Yeah, he wants to buy some stuff, but he talks more about what he wants to fund.

He told me, "I don't want any of my friends to do without. I see people at my school whose families are struggling. I don't ever want anybody around me to struggle. I want to be in a place to help everybody."

Then he starts talking about sowing money to get to that place! At eleven years old!

Ezra has a vision, but now he's interested in finding out the details for how to make it happen

The other day, he got up a little early and came in my prayer room, so we talked for a little bit.

He said, "All right, Dad, you know I'm eleven. I got to know about stocks! Let's get rolling on stocks, Dad. I can't start late in life; I got to get rolling now. I need to know about cryptos, stocks, grow stocks, dividends, and triple leverage. I like those triple-leverage stocks! Let's start talking about this stuff."

Ezra's ready to get rolling, and he wants a well-designed plan.

You should be ready to get rolling too; a well-designed plan will keep you motivated and help you reach your goals.

But how do you get the DETAILS for your design? The story of Nehemiah holds the answer.

Messengers brought Nehemiah a sad report about his hometown, Jerusalem: "The wall of Jerusalem is broken down, and its gates have been burned with fire" (Nehemiah 1:3 NIV).

When Nehemiah heard it, the Bible says he mourned, wept, and fasted for many days.

He now has a strong desire to go to Jerusalem to rebuild the wall, but he's got two big problems: first, he's a captive in Persia, and second, he works as a cupbearer for the Persian king!

It looks like Nehemiah's stuck, doesn't it? It seems like he'll never be able to build the prophetic word in his heart.

Thankfully, a breakthrough is coming. (God always sends a breakthrough for those willing to do the work!)

But this breakthrough doesn't arrive exactly as Nehemiah expects—it comes in the form of a risky opportunity!

In the palace, there was a rule that said no one was supposed to be sad around the king. If you came in with a long face, you could lose your job—or your head! But Nehemiah couldn't help it. He must have had one of those faces that can't hide what he's feeling.

Before long, the king confronts him and asks, "Why is your face sad, since you are not sick? This is nothing but sorrow of heart" (Nehemiah 2:2 NKJV).

When you are carrying a prophetic word, it can show all over you—even to people who don't understand or appreciate it.

I remember the day I had the honor to have dinner with an apostle doing great works. I respect him, so I said, "Apostle, give me something."

He answered, "You know, Joe, apostolic-prophetic people live 20% in the here and now and 80% in the future. How many times in your life have you been talking to somebody and they said, 'Joe, you look spaced out?'"

I said, "Oh, my whole life."

He nodded. "That means you were thinking about the future. When others talk about the past, people like us disengage because we don't go backward; we're always thinking about what's ahead."

So Nehemiah is thinking about his future and can't think of anything else. And now God's giving him the opportunity to talk to the king about it, but he's afraid!

Have you ever felt intimidated when God sends an opportunity YOUR way? Maybe it feels too big for you. Maybe it seems overwhelming. Maybe it triggers your doubts and insecurities or causes your mind to go into overdrive with excuses and negativity.

At that point, it might feel easier to stay in your comfort zone than to walk through the door of opportunity, even if GOD is the one opening the door!

But Nehemiah doesn't have the choice. He can't stay comfortable; he has to answer the king's question!

So he spills out his heart, "May the king live forever! Why should my face not be sad, when the city, the place of my fathers' tombs, lies waste, and its gates are burned with fire?" (Nehemiah 2:3 NIV).

That's pretty bold for Nehemiah, considering he's talking to the Persian king.

But instead of getting angry, the king responds with FAVOR and asks, "What is it you want?" (Nehemiah 2:4 NIV)

Nehemiah answers, "If it pleases the king, and if your servant has found favor in his sight, let him send me to the city in Judah, where my ancestors are buried so that I can rebuild it" (Nehemiah 2:5 NIV).

Nehemiah lays out his vision for the king. He tells him exactly what he wants to do.

And how does the king respond?

He asks for SPECIFICS about Nehemiah's plans! Kings always want to know about the details. (Think about that before you visit a bank without a business plan!)

"Then the king, with the queen sitting beside him, asked me, 'How long will your journey take, and when will you get back?' It pleased the king to send me; so I set a time" (Nehemiah 2:6 NIV).

So, Nehemiah's problem is solved. He's no longer stuck. He can go back to Jerusalem and rebuild the city's walls!

You think he'd be jumping for joy! You think he'd be packing his bags! But Nehemiah's not finished yet.

Remember his days of prayer and fasting?

During that time, he "counted the cost," and he knows what it will take to build.

Since the king is still listening, Nehemiah decides to be bold:

> I also said to him, "If it pleases the king, may I have letters to the governors of Trans-Euphrates, so that they will provide me safe-conduct until I arrive in Judah? 8 And may I have a letter to Asaph, keeper of the royal park, so he will give me timber to make beams for the gates of the citadel by the temple and for the city wall and for the residence I will occupy?" And because the gracious hand of my God was on me, the king granted my requests.
>
> —Nehemiah 2:7-8 NIV

Wait, that's a lot of details for Nehemiah to be rattling off the top of his head!

How did he come up with this elaborate plan so quickly?

Don't you remember? He didn't!

The details didn't come to him when he was standing before the king. They came to him during his days of praying and fasting!

As Nehemiah invested time thinking and praying about what he was going to build, God gave him wisdom.

God helped him design a detailed plan to get the job done!

That's how you'll get the specifics for what you'll build too.

You'll spend time in God's presence.

You'll fast and pray.

You'll fill yourself up with His Word for inspiration.

You'll pray in the spirit for direction.

And you'll download the details—just like Nehemiah did!

My son Ezra is confident he'll get the details of his future financial dream by spending time with me.

You can be confident that you'll get the details of YOUR plan by spending time with God.

Reflection

Scriptures to Think About

Nehemiah 1:4 NIV

When I heard these things, I sat down and wept. For some days I mourned and fasted and prayed before the God of heaven.

Nehemiah 2:2-8 NIV

So the king asked me, "Why does your face look so sad when you are not ill? This can be nothing but sadness of heart." I was very much afraid, but I said to the king, "May the king live forever! Why should my face not look sad when the city where my ancestors are buried lies in ruins, and its gates have been destroyed by fire?"

The king said to me, "What is it you want?"

Then I prayed to the God of heaven, and I answered the king, "If it pleases the king and if your servant has found favor in his sight, let him send me to the city in Judah where my ancestors are buried so that I can rebuild it."

Then the king, with the queen sitting beside him, asked me, "How long will your journey take, and when will you get back?" It pleased the king to send me; so I set a time. And the king granted my requests because the gracious hand of my God was on me.

WITH GOD

You have to push past your current mindset to reach a higher level. You have to push past what you ordinarily do.

CHAPTER 9

IT'S TIME FOR BREAKTHROUGH

One evening recently, the kids were all in different places, and Autumn and I were home alone with our little Cavapoo pup, Lou. We just enjoyed an entire evening of talking and dreaming, and it was so much fun!

Let me ask you, when was the last time you dreamed? When was the last time you got with your spouse, a close friend, or a sibling and just dreamed about life?

When Autumn and I have nights like this, it always refreshes me because we get refocused on the promises of God.

If you don't remind yourself of God's promises, you'll soon lose your ability to dream.

Maybe some of you have started a business, but it didn't work out. God wants you to dream again.

Maybe someone rejected your friendship before. Reach out again.

Maybe you were confident about achieving your goals, but

after some disappointments, you feel inadequate.

You've given up. You're too young. Or too old. You don't have enough money. You're not educated enough. People told you couldn't do it—and you believed them.

Friend, whatever it is that has shut you down, you need to STOP, REFOCUS, and LISTEN to what the Lord is saying.

In this season, you're not just going to dream, but your dreams are coming to pass.

Psalms 130:5 says, "This is why I wait upon you, expecting your breakthrough" (TPT).

Are you expecting a breakthrough? Or are you too distracted by the negativity that surrounds you?

I'll tell you a secret: if you want a breakthrough in your circumstances, you must first experience a breakthrough in your MIND. If you let it, your mind can work against you and shut down your possibilities in God.

The other day, I was riding my mountain bike, and my mind said, "Take it easy, Joe. You're 49. You've had a few surgeries. You don't have to do that next lap. It's hot out."

I live in Texas, and that day, it was 114 degrees at six o'clock in the morning.

But you know what I told my mind? I said, "Shut up! I'm doing that lap, and then I will do another!"

I did it too! And I even sped up my pace!

You have to push past your current mindset to reach a higher level. You have to push yourself beyond what you ordinarily do.

Sometimes, when I read my Bible, I'll go past the chapters I planned that day. Many times, I'll get to the end of my prayer time and pray some more. And I'll often spend a little extra time with my wife or kids.

Whatever it is, you can't let your mind limit you. You need to shatter that glass ceiling and continue believing for a breakthrough.

If you've given up on your circumstances, it's a sure sign that you haven't been focused on the promises in God's Word. As long as you hold onto His Word, you can hold onto hope.

> I long for you more than any watchman would long for the morning light. I will watch and wait for you, O God, throughout the night. O Israel, keep hoping, keep trusting, and keep waiting on the Lord, for he is tenderhearted, kind, and forgiving. He has a thousand ways to set you free!
>
> —Psalm 130:6-7 TPT

I'm getting excited just reading that!

On your best day, you can't even name a thousand ways, but His thoughts are higher than your thoughts, and His ways are higher than your ways. (Isaiah 55:9 NIV)

You don't know how your deliverance is coming. You don't know when your breakthrough will show up. But it's going to happen! He's just going to surprise you. He's going to come through in a way that you couldn't even imagine.

I remember a time I was having a rough week. I don't know if you ever had any of those, but it was intense. But when I refocused and started praying and declaring His Word, I started getting so excited I began to bounce a little!

Then, the Lord said something so clear to me. He said, "You have to pray until you get above the storm."

It made me remember what Big Nanny told me when I was just a young man starting out with God. She said, "You know what the problem is in your generation?"

I said, "What, Big Nanny?"

She said, "You pray until you are through. My generation prayed through! Now get back in there and pray until you pray through!"

"Well, how long will that take, Big Nanny?"

She answered, "Until your attitude changes."

Big Nanny didn't sugarcoat anything!

Like me, you've got to learn how to pray until your attitude changes. You can be in the worst situation of your life but if you stay in tune with the Holy Spirit, you'll still have an abundance of joy. But you've got to be able to pray yourself through.

I invite a guest minister to my church each year, and he always says, "I just pray until I get happy. My wife won't let me come into the house if I'm mad."

You can't let anything steal your joy. You've got to have a strong mindset fixed on the Word.

I encourage you to refocus on the promises of God. They will encourage you and strengthen your thinking.

Listen to Deuteronomy 31:8, "The Lord Himself goes before you and will be with you. He will never leave you nor forsake you. Do not be afraid, nor be discouraged."

If you were raised in a traditional church and then step into a prophetic or apostolic ministry, you will have to break some mental barriers.

If you have a poverty mindset and want to move into prosperity, there are more barriers to break.

If you try to take your health back, you must get a new mindset about your eating and exercise habits.

The Lord will be with you. Don't get discouraged because the Word says He goes before you and will never leave you.

He sees what the future can be if you follow Him, and He speaks it forth and gives you a target to move toward.

Trust in Him and expect your breakthrough!

Reflection

Scripture to Think About

Psalm 130:5-7 TPT

This is why I wait upon you, expecting your breakthrough,
for your Word brings me hope.
I long for you more than any watchman
would long for the morning light.
I will watch and wait for you, O God,
throughout the night.
O Israel, keep hoping, keep trusting,
and keep waiting on the Lord,
for he is tenderhearted, kind, and forgiving.
He has a thousand ways to set you free!

Isaiah 55:9 NKJV

For as the heavens are higher than the earth,
So are My ways higher than your ways,
And My thoughts than your thoughts.

Deuteronomy 31:8 NIV
The Lord himself goes before you and will be with you;
he will never leave you nor forsake you. Do not be afraid;
do not be discouraged.

When that wind of acceleration hits and you're on the right path, you can do in HOURS what it would usually take YEARS to do.

CHAPTER 10

ACCELERATION

A few days ago, I woke up excited. I mean super, super excited. As soon as my eyes opened, I felt God's presence and power in my room.

I've felt that exact feeling several times before, and it always means one thing—we've entered a season of acceleration.

The next day, multiple people from our mentoring and health coaching families started messaging me, saying, "Hey, man, I just feel like things are speeding up. Things are falling into place; things are starting to happen."

I'm experiencing this fast pace in my own life, too. Things are rapidly falling into place in our ministries and businesses.

New opportunities have taken off quickly. There's been a noticeable acceleration.

When you position yourself correctly, you can move quickly when the anointing of the Lord starts flowing on the things you are doing.

The enemy may try to delay or hinder you from fulfilling God's purpose in your life, but I declare in Jesus's name that the spirit of delay is broken over you right now.

God will make up for lost time.

The Lord gave me a vision regarding acceleration. I could see the wind of God moving across the water, pushing the flow of the water in one direction.

A boat was on the water with its sail raised. It was moving with the wind at an accelerated pace. The Lord showed me that the people in this boat had the right mindset and were partnering with Him to build the visions in their hearts.

But there were other boats in this vision with their sails down, and, even crazier, the people in them were rowing their boats AGAINST the wind.

As I kept praying, the Lord said, "There are so many people rowing against My will, favor, blessings, and acceleration. They are determined to go the other way."

Do you know what happens when people go against the wind like that? They wear themselves out and go nowhere.

Think about Jonah. The first time the Lord spoke to him about going to Ninevah to preach, Jonah ran in the opposite direction. Then he had the encounter with the whale, and the whale spit him up on the beach.

Then the Bible records, "Now the word of the Lord came to Jonah for the second time, saying arise, go to Nineveh, the great City, and preach to it the message that I tell you to preach" (Jonah 3:1-3 NIV).

This time, Jonah went!

If God has come to you twice, or even three or four times, I urge you to take advantage of His mercy, quit fighting the wind, and go in the direction He's put in your heart!

I'm telling you that there's an acceleration from God on ALL His promises and purposes for your life you don't want to miss!

Maybe you feel like you've missed your opportunity and that you're stuck rowing against the waves. But I have good news for you, friend:

Our God is the God of second chances!

To you, it feels like it's too late, but for Him, it's never too late.

You've still got time.

I remember one time in my late 20s, it felt like I was going nowhere. I prayed, "God, I feel like everything's moving so slowly. I've missed some things, and I've been overlooked."

The Lord answered, "I'm about to speed you up; I'm about to accelerate you!"

I encourage you to get pointed in the right direction with the Lord, put up your sail, and let the Lord speed you up, too!

When that wind of acceleration hits and you're on the right path, you can do in HOURS what it would usually take YEARS to do. And anything you've lost in the delay, He will restore.

You won't have to speed things up yourself; the Holy Spirit will make it happen.

I declare to you today that the Lord will accelerate your efforts.

Reflection

_____
_____
_____
_____
_____
_____
_____
_____
_____
_____

Scripture to Think About

Jonah 1:1-3 NIV

The word of the Lord came to Jonah son of Amittai: "Go to the great city of Nineveh and preach against it, because its wickedness has come up before me."

But Jonah ran away from the Lord and headed for Tarshish. He went down to Joppa, where he found a ship bound for that port. After paying the fare, he went aboard and sailed for Tarshish to flee from the Lord.

Jonah 3:1 NIV

Then the word of the Lord came to Jonah a second time: "Go to the great city of Nineveh and proclaim to it the message I give you." Jonah obeyed the word of the Lord and went to Nineveh.

Amos 9:13-14 NLT

"The time will come," says the Lord, "when the grain and grapes will grow faster than they can be harvested. Then the terraced vineyards on the hills of Israel will drip with sweet wine! I will bring my exiled people of Israel back from distant lands, and they will rebuild their ruined cities and live in them again. They will plant vineyards and gardens, they will eat their crops and drink their wine.

A Final Note from the Author

As we conclude this book, can I share one last piece of advice? If an idea persists or a dream lingers in your heart, that's the Holy Spirit at work. He thinks it's important enough to keep bringing it to your attention.

Pursuing God's vision for your life may not always feel comfortable, but I promise it will be worth it.

I remember the day I held my first book in my hands. I'll have to admit—I cried. Don't judge me. If you had gone through what I went through to get that first message from heart to paper, you would have shed some tears, too!

But the Lord kept telling me, "It's time to write this book, Joe Joe. It's time to get it out."

Even before my heart was fully confident, He was confident in me. As I now release this newest book, I have a different mindset. Never again will I have to go through what I went through with that initial struggle. That barrier has been broken.

I use my example to encourage you to push past your mental limits, too! If you want to live your best life ever, decide today that you will Build, Create, and Design with God.

Are you interested in mentoring?

For more information about our mentoring program, **Mentored by Joe Joe Dawson,** visit our website:

JoeJoeDawson.net

About the Author

Joe Joe Dawson, the Founder and Apostle of Roar Church Texarkana, is a visionary spiritual leader who is passionate about igniting awakening and revival.

As a transformative mindset mentor and bestselling author of influential books such as 'Kingdom Thinking' and 'Living Your God-Sized Dream,' Joe Joe empowers people to connect with God, shatter the limits of their thinking, and achieve supernatural success.

Beyond the pages of his books, Joe Joe reaches a broad audience through his popular YouTube show 'Joe Joe in the Morning,' where he offers daily encouragement and practical strategies for living 'your best life ever.' His down-to-earth manner and practical spirituality resonate with individuals from all walks of life.

Joe Joe is happily married to the love of his life, Autumn, and together they are raising three exceptional children - Malachi, Judah, and Ezra.

In addition to their ministry, this influential couple owns multiple businesses, including a thriving health coaching venture and the rapidly growing mentorship program, Mentored by Joe Joe Dawson.

Connect with Joe Joe Dawson

JOE JOE DAWSON
Facebook

@JOE_JOE_DAWSONTXK
Instagram

@JoeJoeDawson
YouTube

@PASTORJOEDAWSON
Twitter

JoeJoeDawson
Rumble

JOEJOEDAWSON.NET
Website

Other Books by the Author

Kingdom Thinking
Personal Turnaround
The 40 P's of the Apostolic
Living Your God-Sized Dream
Recipe for Revival
Unworthy But Called
Kingdom Mindset
The Flow
Fast Track
Moving Forward
Voices of Roar
Destiny Dimensions

Made in the USA
Coppell, TX
30 April 2025